COLDER THAN HERE

BY LAURA WADE

D1563575

★

DRAMATISTS
PLAY SERVICE
INC.

SPECIAL NOTE

COLDER THAN HERE was first performed
at Soho Theatre, London, on February 3, 2005,
in a Soho Theatre Production directed by Abigail Morris.

It was subsequently produced by Manhattan Class Company (MCC)
at the Lucille Lortel Theatre, New York, on September 28, 2005,
directed by Abigail Morris.

COLDER THAN HERE received its New York City premiere by Manhattan Class Company (MCC) (John G. Schultz, Executive Director; Robert LuPone, Artistic Director; Bernard Telsey, Artistic Director; William Cantler, Associate Artistic Director) at the Lucille Lortel Theatre, opening on September 28, 2005. It was directed by Abigail Morris; the set design was by Jeff Cowie; the costume design was by Candice Donnelly; the lighting design was by Michael Chybowski; the sound design was by John Leonard; the dialect coach was Stephen Gabis; and the projection design was by Brian H. Kim. The cast was as follows:

MYRA .... Judith Light
ALEC .... Brian Murray
HARRIET .... Sarah Paulson
JENNA .... Lily Rabe

COLDER THAN HERE received its British premiere by Soho Theatre Company at Soho Theatre, London, opening on February 3, 2005. It was directed by Abigail Morris; the set and costume design were by Naomi Wilkinson; the lighting design was by Nigel Edwards; and the sound design was by John Leonard. The cast was as follows:

MYRA .... Margot Leicester
ALEC .... Michael Pennington
HARRIET .... Georgia Mackenzie
JENNA .... Anna Madeley

CHARACTERS

A FAMILY:

MYRA — aged 56
ALEC — aged 57
HARRIET — aged 29
JENNA — aged 27

SETTING

The action moves between the living room of the Bradley family home in Leamington Spa, and various woodland/greenfield burial sites around the West Midlands.

COLDER THAN HERE

Scene 1

A burial ground in the West Midlands. Midday. Mid-September — almost autumn but still warm enough not to wear a coat or carry an umbrella. The site is young, the trees just a few years old and still spindly. There are no headstones — graves are marked by shrubs or trees with the occasional wooden plaque. Myra stands looking around her. She is noticeably thin but surprisingly energetic. She is suffering from advanced secondary bone cancer, but today has little pain. Jenna, her daughter, aged twenty-seven, stands a little way off, a large picnic basket beside her. She wears mostly black, with a long stripy scarf.

MYRA. Here.
JENNA. Here?
MYRA. Yes, I think so. Don't you think so?
JENNA. I'm not — I don't know.
MYRA. I think here is good. Flattest bit. Under a tree — I like that, nice and shady. Let's say here. *(Myra indicates an area on the ground.)*
JENNA. Fine. *(Myra looks at Jenna. Jenna doesn't move.)*
MYRA. Yes?
JENNA. Fine. *(Jenna looks around.)*
MYRA. Bring the basket over.
JENNA. You want to eat here?
MYRA. Yes.
JENNA. You want to eat. Here.
MYRA. Yes, let's eat, you'll eat here lots. It's out of the sun, it's …
JENNA. It's *morbid.*
MYRA. It's happening, Jen, come on. *(Jenna brings the picnic bas-*

5

ket over. Myra opens the basket and pulls out a large blanket, which she starts to shake out. Jenna looks away.)

JENNA. Did you see the. Did you see the baby?

MYRA. No.

JENNA. There's a baby. Under some holly, a holly bush.

MYRA. That's lovely. Never dies, that's lovely. *(Myra is struggling with the blanket.)* Could you, um?

JENNA. Yeh. *(They lay out the blanket together.)*

MYRA. Was there a marker?

JENNA. Two months old.

MYRA. Can't say that's a good innings, can you? *(Myra sits down and starts unpacking the picnic.)* Now. Plates … Are you warm enough?

JENNA. Fine. *(Myra pulls out two plastic plates. She hands one to Jenna. Jenna holds it like it smells bad.)*

MYRA. Um, forks … *(Hands a plastic fork to Jenna.)* Napkins … *(Hands a napkin to Jenna.)*

JENNA. Mum, I don't need a —

MYRA. Have a napkin.

JENNA. I don't want a / napkin.

MYRA. Have a napkin. *(Jenna takes it.)*

JENNA. Serviette. *(A look.)* Basket smells funny.

MYRA. Found it in the cellar. *(Jenna looks at Myra.)* I wiped it, it's fine. Everything's in plastic, it'll taste fine. *(Myra looks into the basket.)* I brought things you like.

JENNA. I don't want anything.

MYRA. Sausage rolls, I've got sandwiches, posh crisps, jaffa cakes, quiche, you might turn your nose up at / that —

JENNA. Bloody hell, Mum, this lot don't eat anymore, you know.

MYRA. You're picky. Lots of / options.

JENNA. You're not supposed to be cooking and — *(Myra starts to pull food out of the hamper.)*

MYRA. I didn't. Marks. Jaffa cakes might be a bit own-brand. Lots of sandwiches.

JENNA. I don't like sandwiches.

MYRA. You don't — Since when?

JENNA. I woke up one morning and realised I'd been living a lie all my life.

MYRA. Oh for God's / sake.

JENNA. I'm bored of them. They're always soggy, people put too much stuff in them, they're impossible to eat.

6

MYRA. Sausage roll? *(Jenna raises her eyebrows.)* Vegetarian sausage roll.

JENNA. Not a sausage roll, then, is it? *(Jenna takes a sausage roll and starts to pick at it.)*

MYRA. Know what I hate about sandwiches? When people say the D. SANDwiches.

JENNA. SANDwiches. Samwidge.

MYRA. Exactly. Not SANDwich. *(Jenna looks around her, eating her sausage roll.)* There isn't one.

JENNA. One what?

MYRA. Toilet. You're looking for a toilet to go to after you eat that.

JENNA. I'm not. *(A look.)* I don't. Mum, I don't.

MYRA. How would I know?

JENNA. I don't do that anymore. *(Myra opens a sandwich and starts to eat it.)* There is one, anyway.

MYRA. Jen—

JENNA. What? Just a point of information — there's one by the caretaker's house. I happened to see it on the way in.

MYRA. You were looking.

JENNA. No, I just — we were driving in and I saw it and I thought, "Oh, a toilet, you need a toilet, all the old biddies that come here." It's not a toilet I want to yak into. *(Myra looks intently at Jenna.)* It's a habit, isn't it? You get used to all the little — Things you do kind of around the main thing, even when you stop doing the thing you still have the little — habits.

MYRA. So eat that properly. *(Jenna stuffs the whole sausage roll into her mouth and looks at Myra, challenging. Swallowing takes longer than she expects and she turns away, breaking the look.)*

JENNA. That was next-*level* disgusting.

MYRA. Another one? The sandwiches aren't bad, not soggy / really.

JENNA. Every time I see you do I have to stuff my face just to / prove I'm —

MYRA. I got some hummus ones.

JENNA. Fine.

MYRA. Do you like it?

JENNA. Hummus?

MYRA. Here. Do you think we should bury me here.

JENNA. I don't want to bury you anywhere.

MYRA. That was almost affectionate.

JENNA. I don't like —

MYRA. It's just that we haven't got long.

JENNA. How long?

MYRA. Six months or so. Up to about nine.

JENNA. Jesus. *(Beat.)* Does it — Does it hurt?

MYRA. Just aches and pains. I've started to make a noise when I bend down to pick things up.

JENNA. Like what?

MYRA. Kind of "Uhh." "Uhh." Like an old lady. *(Beat. Jenna fumbles in her bag and takes out her cigarettes.)* Mind you, your dad does that already, I might just have picked it up off — So you're smoking in front of your mother now?

JENNA. Won't have a chance soon, will I?

MYRA. You giving up? *(A look. Jenna puts the cigarettes away.)* You learned to smoke in a graveyard, didn't you? You and that boy from the comprehensive — *(Jenna looks at her.)* What, you think we didn't — You came home covered in lichen, smelling of mints and Impulse. Of course we knew about it. Why I asked you to come, prior knowledge. Haven't told Alec yet. We always said cremation but now it — Think he might find it a bit odd. Cardboard coffin, no headstone or —

JENNA. Cardboard?

MYRA. Or wicker, you can get wicker ones. *(Jenna looks at the picnic basket.)* Yes, alright. Cardboard ones come flatpack. Self-assembly. You could help.

JENNA. You're kidding, right?

MYRA. No.

JENNA. That's fucked up. Next-*level* fucked up, I'm not doing that.

MYRA. Have a think about it.

JENNA. *(Under her breath.)* Fucked up. *(Pause. Myra eats a sandwich.)*

MYRA. Maybe plant a holly bush.

JENNA. Does Harriet know?

MYRA. No.

JENNA. Sounds like one of hers.

MYRA. I read a book. You have to find things to do. When you're off work with dying. Leamington Library's got loads of death books, shelves and shelves of cancer. And then this one saying you can be buried somewhere pretty if you want to. Hadn't even thought about it … Harri had nothing to do with it. I wanted to tell you.

JENNA. Tell her everything else first. *(Beat.)*

MYRA. You had a lot to deal with / at the time.

JENNA. Like what?

MYRA. You'd just got together with Mark. You were — busy.

JENNA. You'd been to three appointments before anyone said anything.

MYRA. We didn't want to worry you. You worry.

JENNA. It was important and I missed it. "Hello love, just had my thyroid gland whipped out, how's the new boyfriend?"

MYRA. Does it matter, Jen? Does it really matter. Now. *(Pause.)*

JENNA. Can I have a jaffa cake, please? *(Myra hands her the packet. Jenna stands up and walks around, the packet of jaffa cakes in her hand. She eats one.)*

MYRA. Rowan tree, maybe?

JENNA. Ugh, squishy berries.

MYRA. Cherry. Flowering cherry. Just blossom, nothing squishy.

JENNA. Palm tree, get some fucking monkeys …

MYRA. How are they?

JENNA. All right. Chocolate's a bit baggy. *(Jenna looks out at the traditional cemetery over the fence.)* Why do they have the lawny bit there and then this bit here?

MYRA. Give you a choice?

JENNA. So ugly, all laid out in straight rows, shiny marble, plastic fucking buckets. Someone should go 'round and take the dead flowers off, looks a fucking mess.

MYRA. This bit's nicer.

JENNA. Have to walk through the plastic buckets to get to you, though.

MYRA. Perhaps you could tell him for me, the burial thing.

JENNA. Oh Mum, I —

MYRA. I mean there may come a time when you two need to learn to talk to each other …

JENNA. We talk.

MYRA. Not really.

JENNA. We get on fine, we don't argue.

MYRA. No, it's a shame. Give you a reason to come 'round and see us. Haven't seen you properly in months, when did you last sit and chat to him? *(Jenna eats another jaffa cake.)*

JENNA. Dad doesn't like me.

MYRA. Of course he likes you, he loves you.

JENNA. He doesn't *like* me.

MYRA. He doesn't like Mark very much.

JENNA. Yeah, well. He didn't mean to be rude, he's just — That's Mark, I don't know. Don't think I like him much right now. *(Jenna*

9

continues to eat jaffa cakes as she talks.) Wants to quit work and do a university course 'cause he says it's too much of a strain working in the same shop every day 'cause we end up spending so much time together, which is stupid it's not like we live together is it, but if I won't leave then he'll have to or we'll end up splitting up. Which I think is going to happen anyway 'cause he's flirting with the manager every day and when I question it he says I'm paranoid or possessive or — And he's just. Being a wanker. And —

MYRA. And?

JENNA. Oh, you know. Love him. Twat.

MYRA. How's the sex?

JENNA. What?

MYRA. How is it?

JENNA. The / sex?

MYRA. Yes.

JENNA. I don't — I'm not talking about that with you, we don't talk about that.

MYRA. Maybe we should.

JENNA. Why?

MYRA. I've never managed to get to the bottom of this relationship you're so disastrously having, and we've. We've never had a talk. It's important / isn't it?

JENNA. Mum, I don't want to —

MYRA. Isn't it? *(Beat.)*

JENNA. You and Daddy don't have sex.

MYRA. How do you know?

JENNA. You've slept in separate rooms for years.

MYRA. You've moved out, how do you know what goes on?

JENNA. So what, you're at it all over the house usually, are you? Then when me and Harri come home you move back into separate bedrooms just to keep us feeling secure in the pair of you not fancying each other ... *(Beat. Myra looks at her watch.)*

MYRA. Tablet time. Would you pass the bottle? *(Jenna takes a bottle of water from the picnic basket and passes it to Myra. She watches Myra take a bottle of tablets out of her bag, put one in her mouth and swallow it down with a drink of water.)*

JENNA. Sorry. *(Jenna puts the jaffa cakes back in the basket.)*

MYRA. While I'm still here I can help. After I kick it you're on your own. *(Myra coughs and drinks more water. Jenna watches her.)* Ugh, too big these ones. What?

JENNA. Nothing. I. Sorry. *(Jenna looks around her.)*

MYRA. So we're happy with here, yes?
JENNA. Sure. *(Beat.)* Actually, no. I think it's a bit —
MYRA. Yes.
JENNA. I think we could find somewhere. Better. *(Myra smiles. Fade.)*

Scene 2

The living room of Myra's family home. Mid-evening, late October. A sofa and an armchair that have been in the same place for many years, newspapers and books in a pile by the armchair. Myra sits on the sofa, working at a laptop on the coffee table in front of her. She wears warm clothes and has a large glass of white wine next to her. There is a half-finished bottle of wine and a couple more glasses. Myra's daughter Harriet is standing behind the sofa taking her coat off.

MYRA. How was it?
HARRIET. Good. It was good. Dad got cross 'cause someone clapped after the second movement.
MYRA. Were they shot?
HARRIET. Social death. Exclusion from the Brahms fan club …
(Pointing at the wine glass.) Should you be —
MYRA. Yes. Emphatically yes. *(A look.)* Shut up. Where's Alec?
HARRIET. Loo. What's this?
MYRA. PowerPoint. You going to stay for a drink?
HARRIET. Yes, short one, Josh'll be waiting up. Why you doing PowerPoint? *(Myra gets a glass and pours wine for Harriet. She uses both hands to lift the bottle.)*
MYRA. Had it sat on the desktop for years, didn't even know what it was. Thought I'd give it a go now I'm never going to work again … I'm bored, Harri. *(Myra laughs.)* Feel like going back.
HARRIET. Get better first, yeah? *(Myra looks at Harriet. Harriet looks away.)*
MYRA. I'm making a presentation.
HARRIET. Show me. *(Alec comes in, polishing his glasses with a lens cloth. He has already taken his coat off.)*
MYRA. Next time. Not ready yet. *(To Alec.)* How was it?

11

ALEC. The cellist was awful.

HARRIET. Dad, she wasn't / awful.

ALEC. She was awful.

HARRIET. Her dress was awful. *(To Myra.)* Big turquoise mermaidy thing. Looked like a burglar's dog.

MYRA. Drink, Alec? *(Alec looks at the wine.)*

ALEC. Yes. Just get some red. *(Alec goes into the kitchen to fetch red wine.)*

MYRA. But nice father-daughter evening?

HARRIET. Yes. And we bought tickets for next time. *(Myra smiles.)* Mahler.

MYRA. That's brave. *(Alec comes back with a bottle of red wine and a glass.)*

HARRIET. Now is it me or is it cold in here?

MYRA. Boiler's on the blink. What? *(Harriet is looking at Alec, smiling.)*

HARRIET. We were playing "phrases Dad hates."

ALEC. "Is it me or is it cold in here." Completely moronic.

HARRIET. What was the other / one?

ALEC. Can't remember. *(Harriet thinks.)*

HARRIET. "A propos of."

ALEC. Well that's just stupid, isn't it? — the "of" is implied in the "a propos," it's *there*. Some chump in the interval, shouting his mouth off ...

MYRA. You shouldn't see people dear, it makes you cross.

HARRIET. What's wrong with the boiler?

ALEC. Not boiling anything. *(Alec picks up a newspaper and opens it, obscuring his face.)*

MYRA. Sore point.

HARRIET. Any news on Baggins?

MYRA. Gone for good, I think.

HARRIET. Have you told her? *(Myra shakes her head, drinks some wine.)*

ALEC. *(From behind the newspaper.)* Sore point.

MYRA. Speaking of sore, we've got another hot spot from the scan last week.

HARRIET. Where? *(Myra points to her left upper arm.)*

MYRA. Humerus. Great name for a bone. So that's four places.

HARRIET. I'm sorry, Mum.

MYRA. Alright, feeling quite sanguine today.

ALEC. Pff. *(Harriet looks at Alec, then at Myra.)*

MYRA. I gave the boiler a good kick this morning ...

HARRIET. Sorry I couldn't come with you. I wanted to come to all of them.

MYRA. Turns out you get extra cloying sympathy if you go on your own.

HARRIET. I hope you were nice. They're professionals.

MYRA. Anyway, a couple more places and we'll be able to say I'm riddled with it.

HARRIET. What are they going to do?

MYRA. More radio. Painkillers. Warm baths. Funeral planning.

HARRIET. Don't be — Mum — *(Myra raises her eyebrows. Drinks. Harriet looks over at Alec, who is immobile behind his newspaper.)* Dad.

ALEC. Yes.

HARRIET. Mum's dying and you're sitting there reading the paper.

ALEC. Watched pot never boils, love. *(Myra laughs, nearly chokes on her wine.)*

HARRIET. Dad!

MYRA. I like that.

HARRIET. Honestly.

MYRA. It's easier if you find the / funny, believe me. *(The front door opens, offstage.)*

JENNA. *(Off.)* Hello. *(Myra, Alec and Harriet look at each other. Jenna comes into the living room, a large sports bag slung over her shoulder. She stands just inside the door, hesitant.)* Hi. *(Myra, Alec and Harriet all look at her. Jenna swings the bag onto the floor.)* What?

MYRA. Is everything alright?

JENNA. I, um. Thought I might. Stay for a bit. If that's — If that's OK.

MYRA. Have you and Mark had an argument?

JENNA. No. No more than usual. It's all fine, he's fine. *(Myra, Alec and Harriet continue to stare at Jenna.)* What? Is this. Is this not alright?

MYRA. Of course it's —

JENNA. All looking at me like it's —

MYRA. It's lovely to see you. *(Jenna puts her hands in her pockets.)* Glass of wine?

JENNA. If it's not too much tr—

MYRA. White or red? *(Jenna looks at Alec's glass.)*

JENNA. Red. *(Myra goes to pick up the bottle and Harriet stops her.)*

HARRIET. Here, let me. *(Jenna watches Harriet. Then Myra.)*

MYRA. Harri and Dad went to the concert tonight. *(Harriet pours a glass of wine for Jenna and hands it to her. Alec goes back to his paper.)*

JENNA. Was it good?

HARRIET. / Yeah.

ALEC. No.

JENNA. What was it?

HARRIET. The Brahms double.

JENNA. I like Brahms.

HARRIET. Since when?

JENNA. "Hungarian Dances" — I like that. The one Dad likes.

MYRA. Brahms! *(Myra types something into the laptop.)*

ALEC. What are you doing?

MYRA. "Hungarian Dances," brilliant. Upbeat. You should take Jenna to a concert sometime. *(Myra continues to type.)*

JENNA. That would be — Um, yeah. *(The others are watching Myra. Jenna pulls her sleeves over her wrists. She moves a little closer to Myra.)* Fucking cold in here.

HARRIET. Boiler's packed up.

JENNA. Oh.

HARRIET. Still want to stay?

JENNA. Course. Yeah. *(Jenna drinks some wine. Harriet watches her from the sofa. Alec reads and Myra types.)* I'll go put my bag — *(Jenna goes to leave with her bag. She doubles back and hugs Myra over the back of the sofa, then leaves rapidly. The others look at each other.)*

HARRIET. God knows. D'you think they've —

MYRA. What, split up? *(Alec takes his shoes off.)*

ALEC. Entrance wasn't dramatic enough.

HARRIET. *(To Myra.)* She'll tell you. *(Jenna returns and stands by the door.)*

JENNA. Ummm …

ALEC. Ah, the ominous um. *(Alec takes his slippers from beside the chair and puts them on. He puts shoe trees in the shoes he has taken off.)*

JENNA. Um, where's Baggins?

ALEC. Ah. *(Alec looks at Myra.)*

JENNA. What?

MYRA. Baggins isn't here.

JENNA. God, he didn't get run over again, did he? *(Myra puts her hands together in her lap.)*

MYRA. No.

JENNA. What, is he — Has he gone on holiday?

HARRIET. Sort of.

JENNA. What? *(Myra motions to Harriet to fill up her wine glass.)*

MYRA. He's um. He's moved out.

JENNA. How — How can he have — He's a cat.

MYRA. They're autonomous, love. It's up to them.

JENNA. He's been here fifteen years, this is his home.

ALEC. Went off with another woman. *(Jenna looks at Myra.)*

MYRA. Alec. He disappeared. Few weeks ago. So I. I put a card in the newsagents with his picture, the phone number and. And the next day a lady rang from Kenilworth Road and said she'd — Got him. She'd been looking after him, thought he was a stray.

JENNA. He's got a collar.

MYRA. Lost it. She wasn't to know.

JENNA. Fucking cat thief.

ALEC. Cat burglar.

MYRA. Alec. She'd only just moved here and her cat died. I felt sorry for her.

JENNA. You left him there?

ALEC. Course she didn't.

MYRA. We went to get him, with the basket. Kept him inside a few days so he'd readjust and it was fine. Then, how long was it?

ALEC. A week. Thereabouts.

MYRA. Went off again.

JENNA. But you went — You went and got him again?

MYRA. Yes. And the time after that. By the fourth time I thought. Well I thought maybe he, he likes it there. Maybe. So I said —

JENNA. What?

MYRA. I said she could keep him.

JENNA. He's my cat. *(Myra taps her fingernails on her wine glass. Jenna wraps her arms around herself.)*

HARRIET. You weren't the one looking after him, Jen.

JENNA. Fuck off being fucking reasonable. I'd have taken him if he'd — If I'd been allowed pets in my flat — we can't all afford to buy our own flat, it's not my fault.

MYRA. We had to let him go.

ALEC. Like the lion in *Born Free.*

MYRA. Alec. If he didn't want to be with us …

JENNA. Did you change the brand of cat food? *(Myra looks at Alec.)* Did you?

MYRA. No. No. *(Jenna goes out to the kitchen.)*

ALEC. My fault.

MYRA. It's not.

HARRIET. It's no one's fault. *(Jenna returns, a can of cat food in*

15

her hand.)

JENNA. He doesn't like this sort. He's never liked this sort. Last time we got this he tried to throw himself under a lorry.

HARRIET. That was completely / disconnected.

JENNA. He doesn't like this.

MYRA. I'm sorry. Your dad's been doing the shopping. I haven't been. Up to it … *(Jenna bites her lip.)* I should have told him which sort to get. *(Pause.)* He might be — Baggins might be better off there, anyway. He's used to having people around, and once I'm — There'll just be your dad here and … *(Long pause.)*

JENNA. *(Under her breath.)* Fuck. *(Harriet looks at Jenna.)* What? *(Harriet looks away, pours more wine. Another long pause. No eye contact: four people alone. Myra drinks, then stands up.)*

MYRA. OK, let's do it now.

HARRIET. What?

MYRA. Shall we look at my presentation?

HARRIET. You said it wasn't ready.

MYRA. It's not really, but since we're all together — doesn't happen much, does it? Family time.

ALEC. What's this?

MYRA. Can you come and sit over here between your daughters, please?

ALEC. Not taking a photograph, are you?

HARRIET. Mum's made a PowerPoint thing.

JENNA. A what?

MYRA. Alec, come and sit over here.

ALEC. I'm reading the — *(A look.)* Alright. *(Alec stands up and sits down gingerly between the two daughters on the sofa.)* What are we looking at?

MYRA. The computer.

ALEC. Need my glasses. *(He's left them on his armchair. He stands up and fetches them.)*

MYRA. Can't you just —

ALEC. Just a second … *(Alec sits back down on the sofa.)* Right.

MYRA. Jenna, you'll have to be my techno person, alright?

JENNA. I don't usually use a —

MYRA. You just have to hit Return when I say, OK?

JENNA. OK.

HARRIET. D'you know which Return is?

JENNA. Not a fucking / clue.

MYRA. Oh, for God's sake, how can you not — / Even I know —

16

HARRIET. That one.

JENNA. Thanks.

MYRA. OK, are we ready? *(The others nod in assent.)* So this is something I've made to. Talk to you about something that — Well, it speaks for itself really. But it's a first draft so — OK. Jenna?

JENNA. Yes?

MYRA. OK?

JENNA. Oh right. *(Jenna presses return. She turns to Myra.)* Is that what you're going to say? When I have to press it.

MYRA. I'll say "Jenna."

JENNA. OK. *(Jenna turns back to the screen, which Alec and Harriet are looking at, aghast. The words "MY FUNERAL, by MYRA BRADLEY" have appeared. The slides also appear on the back wall, behind the family. Alec looks at Myra.)*

ALEC. Myra —

MYRA. So I've been thinking about this and how I want to shuffle off. And. I think it's important for you to know. So you don't get it wrong. So we can plan. OK, Jenna. *(Myra smiles at Alec. Jenna hits return.)*

ALEC. I don't —

MYRA. So if you could just listen. Watch. *(Alec looks back at the screen. The words "No funeral director or mortician" slide onto the screen from the right. With a swooshing noise.)* You can make it do all sorts of things — moving and noises and — So I want us to arrange it. Not a man in a tailcoat. *(A clipart picture has appeared beside the caption.)*

JENNA. Is that a bridegroom?

MYRA. There isn't a funeral director, I told you it's a first draft.

ALEC. You can't do it without an undertaker, it's not legal / is it?

MYRA. It is. There's a guidebook, handbook thing. Death certificates, it's all there. Jenna. *(Jenna hits return. The caption "Woodland burial" slides on from the left. A tree appears with a twinkling sound.)* I'd like to be buried in a —

ALEC. Buried?

MYRA. Yes.

ALEC. Not cremated.

MYRA. No.

ALEC. But we've always — I mean it's, it's in the wills —

MYRA. I'm rewriting mine.

JENNA. It's, um. Cremation's bad. For the environment. It's a pollutant. *(Alec looks at Jenna.)*

MYRA. So I want to be buried in a woodland or a nice field. Jenna and I went to see one last month. Jenna's going to be head of the burial site committee, help me find somewhere just right so —

HARRIET. Jenna is?

MYRA. Yes. We'll need suggestions for a tree to plant on top of me, that would be helpful. Most of these places you can't have a marker. Jenna. *(Jenna hits Return. The caption "Cardboard Coffin" appears on the screen with a fanfare. Beat.)*

ALEC. Cardboard?

MYRA. They're very strong. Much cheaper.

ALEC. Not the point.

MYRA. They come flatpack — we could order it ahead of time. You can paint them. I'd like to paint it. *(Alec goes to speak, but can't.)* Jenna. *(Jenna hits Return. The caption "I will paint. Pillows & plastic liner" slides down from the top of the screen.)* OK, we've talked about that already. Next one, Jen. I haven't put noises on this bit yet ... *(Jenna hits Return. "Bury me in warm clothes." appears, sliding down from the top again, followed by "Velvet scarf. My big red shawl.")* I'm thinking it might be cold down there. Jenna. *(Jenna hits Return. "Coffin to be carried by family" appears from the lower part of the screen.)* Perhaps not you, Alec, not with your back. *(Alec takes his glasses off and puts them on the table. He leans back. Harriet drinks her wine.)* It's all a bit sketchy here — just ideas I threw down. Jenna, just page through them. *(Jenna hits Return at short intervals and we see the following appear: "Springtime flowers — depends on how long I last.")* So I guess we won't know about that for a while ... *(The next caption "No throwing flowers.")* Looks a bit shoddy, doesn't it? Sounds funny, flowers thudding on the ... *(Then, next to "No throwing flowers" appears " — throw something else," then, a moment later "Glitter?")* OK, so that's a bit silly. There should be something like confetti we could use. *(Alec shifts in his seat. The next caption: "No Astroturf," followed shortly by "For god's sake.")*

HARRIET. Astroturf?

MYRA. You know at funerals when they cover up the earth by the side of the grave with fake grass? Like being buried in a greengrocers. Jenna, next one? *(Jenna hits Return. The caption "Watch grave being filled" appears.)*

ALEC. What the —

MYRA. I think you should all stay there and watch while they fill it up.

ALEC. Oh, this is — No, excuse me. *(Alec stands up, moves away from the sofa.)*

MYRA. I don't want everybody strolling away, leaving me …

JENNA. I feel sick. Feel a bit sick.

HARRIET. You knew about this?

JENNA. Not all of it.

ALEC. We're not going to — This is too —

MYRA. What, love, what?

ALEC. We're not —

MYRA. It's my funeral.

ALEC. Funny.

MYRA. Why can't I make jokes about it, isn't that how we — *(Pause.)* Please, Alec, we have to —

ALEC. We're not. We're not burying you in a. Cardboard box. *(Alec leaves.)*

MYRA. Alec. It doesn't go away if we don't — *(The others are silent for a moment.)*

JENNA. Left his glasses. Have to come back down. *(They look at the glasses.)*

HARRIET. Could take them up. I can't believe you knew about this, why didn't you —

JENNA. I don't know, I —

HARRIET. You just don't *think*, do you? *(Harriet picks up Alec's glasses and follows him out. Myra stares at the coffee table. Jenna looks after Harriet and Alec.)*

MYRA. I want it decorated with the sky and the stars. *(Fade.)*

Scene 3

Another burial ground near Leamington. This is a level meadow with wild flowers and long grasses during the summer, but now, on a wintry Saturday in mid-November, looks a little bleak. Harriet and Jenna stand facing each other by a wooden stile. Harriet holds her lunch — couscous salad in a Tupperware box — which she will continue to eat in a moment.

HARRIET. What, she didn't tell you?

19

JENNA. What?

HARRIET. She's feeling a bit — Um, yeah.

JENNA. Bit what?

HARRIET. Bit cancerous. Asked if I'd come instead.

JENNA. She was fine when I left this morning.

HARRIET. Maybe she —

JENNA. Well, that's a fat lot of bloody good, isn't it, we're not burying you.

HARRIET. She didn't want to leave you stranded. And your mobile's switched off. *(Jenna forages for her phone in her handbag, and eventually pulls it out.)*

JENNA. Fuck. Always forget to frigging — Forget to fucking lock it …

HARRIET. Anyway, nice to see you, thanks for coming.

JENNA. Thanks. *(They look out across the field.)*

HARRIET. Not up to much, is it?

JENNA. No.

HARRIET. D'you pick this?

JENNA. It's in the book.

HARRIET. Hmm. *(Harriet eats.)* God, my boyfriend's a good cook. We were just having lunch, put some in a box for me, bless him. D'you want some?

JENNA. No thanks.

HARRIET. 'S really good.

JENNA. Hate the smell of Tupperware. This family. Always eating in fucking cemeteries. *(Harriet eats, Jenna surveys the field.)* Did you hear it arrived yesterday?

HARRIET. Did it?

JENNA. Great big flatpack thing. Postman made some funny about enormous packages, not being able to get it through the letter box …

HARRIET. Who answered the door?

JENNA. Dad.

HARRIET. Great.

JENNA. Then there's a hoo-haa about where to put it. Dad said it should go in the cellar, then Mum says it'd get too damp. So then Dad wanders off muttering it'll get a lot damper once it's used …

HARRIET. Where is it now?

JENNA. Behind the sofa. Wants to build it straight away, try it out for size. So we can all get used to it. Apparently if we see it around the place we won't be so upset when she's in it.

HARRIET. Just start sleeping in it, freak us out properly … *(Beat. They look around.)* Well, I'm glad we didn't drag her all this way, are you? *(Jenna goes to sit on the lower bench of the stile.)* I mean, how would we know where she was? You'll get a wet arse.

JENNA. Don't care.

HARRIET. It's a bit damp. *(Harriet looks in her rucksack and pulls out a carrier bag.)* D'you want a bag?

JENNA. No thanks. *(Harriet spreads out the plastic bag on the upper step of the stile and sits down.)*

HARRIET. You wouldn't know, would you? You'd have to remember, there's no markers or anything. 'Less they buried her right by the wall. Can't say I like the idea of having to find my mother with a map and a compass. *(Beat.)*

JENNA. Do you miss her?

HARRIET. Do I miss her?

JENNA. Like when people say "missing you already" when they're saying goodbye. I miss her already.

HARRIET. Thought I'd wait till she's gone, myself. *(Jenna takes her cigarettes from her pocket and lights one.)* Oh please not here.

JENNA. These places. Give me a death wish.

HARRIET. Do you have to?

JENNA. Yes, I'm addicted. That's what addiction is.

HARRIET. Don't blow it on my lunch. How many have you had today?

JENNA. Umpteen. *(Beat.)* I miss her. Like the other day, that day I came home when you were there, I'd been really missing her. Got home from work and it was a shit day and — I. Wanted her there. And I got home and. Just gripped by it. Desperately wanted her. Lying in bed, crying my eyes out and there's no one else, no one else is good enough. *(Harriet stops eating. She looks across the field, away from Jenna, frowning.)* Kind of frightening, getting this, "I want my mummy." Hadn't felt that for years, I mean when did you last feel that, your whole body?

HARRIET. I. I can't remember.

JENNA. So *basic*, like the cord or something, being pulled out from — *(Mimes a cord coming out of her stomach.)* Yeah.

HARRIET. What did you do?

JENNA. Can't cry all day, can you, you run out. Packed a bag and went 'round to Mum's.

HARRIET. Did you tell her?

JENNA. 'Course not. But now I keep thinking about next time I

21

feel like … You ever get days when just breathing too deeply makes you cry? *(Beat.)*

HARRIET. How long are you planning to stay? At home.

JENNA. Don't know.

HARRIET. 'Cause it seems you've pretty much moved back in.

JENNA. Plenty of time for living in a shit flat on my own when she's —

HARRIET. Don't you think — Don't you think maybe they need some time. Just them? *(Jenna stands up.)*

JENNA. I have got a wet arse now.

HARRIET. Don't you think?

JENNA. She'd ask.

HARRIET. Come on, she couldn't ask that.

JENNA. Why not?

HARRIET. Because you'd react like you always do.

JENNA. Like / what?

HARRIET. Like everything's your tragedy and no one / else's.

JENNA. I don't — I don't always — I'm having a really shitty time right now in case you hadn't —

HARRIET. See? You see? This is — This is it exactly.

JENNA. What?

HARRIET. You're *always* having a shitty time. You're this fragile little spiky tissue paper thing we're s'posed to all look after and if we have to cancel holidays 'cause you've got dumped or if we have to rush off to hospital in the night 'cause you've got too happy with the alcopops and. And 'cause it's you, you don't just get sick and go to sleep you get fucking convulsions, or we have to spend every family meal not talking about boyfriends 'cause you're always about to break up with one, and trying not to notice when you dash straight upstairs straight after pudding then — And now Mum's disappearing and you're still fucking about like — Like it's your disaster. It's not about you now. You haven't been to the hospital once.

JENNA. I'm scared of hospitals. Mum knows.

HARRIET. Maybe I'm scared of burial grounds. Well, here I fucking am.

JENNA. When did you start swearing?

HARRIET. Only swear when I'm really fucked off. *(Jenna looks away. Pause.)*

JENNA. We going to come here and argue once we've buried her, d'you think?

HARRIET. We're not burying her here. It's too bleak.

JENNA. Yeah, it is. *(Beat.)* Isn't even a bloody loo. *(Beat.)* Sorry. It's hard, you know?

HARRIET. Yeah.

JENNA. And I'm not. I'm not strong. You're strong.

HARRIET. Yeah. *(Jenna sniffs.)*

JENNA. Have you got a — *(Harriet pulls a tissue out of her bag and hands it to her.)* Thanks. *(Jenna blows her nose. Harriet puts the lid back on her Tupperware box and presses it down firmly at each corner. Jenna watches her.)* D'you and Josh ever fight? *(Harriet sighs.)*

HARRIET. Is this leading into a Mark / discussion —

JENNA. No.

HARRIET. Because you know I think you should / dump —

JENNA. I just want to know if you guys ever —

HARRIET. Not everyone wants to be yelling all the time —

JENNA. I don't want to, we just seem to —

HARRIET. So dump him just do it. *(Beat.)*

JENNA. You never fight?

HARRIET. Sometimes. Rare occasions.

JENNA. About what?

HARRIET. Stupid things. Little things. Just when we're both stressed and.

JENNA. You start bitching at each other and it blows up —

HARRIET. Not like that, no. Just like, I don't know — I don't know why I'm having to justify my relationship here — like when we were buying the house and we both really wanted it and we were scared we wouldn't get it, so. I'd go off at him about things he should have done and he'd get cross at me 'cause I didn't understand how busy he is and how he was trying to earn lots of money so we could afford it …

JENNA. How do they end?

HARRIET. I go all quiet, he hugs me and we both feel better and get on with it.

JENNA. D'you have sex afterwards?

HARRIET. Jen.

JENNA. Mum thinks we should talk about sex more.

HARRIET. Mum thinks we should spend time together. *(Beat.)* I think she switched your phone off deliberately.

JENNA. She couldn't have —

HARRIET. You never check it. She could have done it this morning. When you were in the shower or something.

JENNA. I don't —

HARRIET. I might be wrong.

JENNA. Never.

HARRIET. Piss off.

JENNA. How long after the fight d'you make up?

HARRIET. What?

JENNA. How long afterwards?

HARRIET. Half an hour?

JENNA. Same day.

HARRIET. Always. *(Jenna frowns and looks across the field.)*

JENNA. D'you think we've given it long enough now?

HARRIET. I think we've established this isn't it.

JENNA. This is not it.

HARRIET. She wouldn't like it.

JENNA. I think trees are the thing. Did you see the lady at the office?

HARRIET. Said hello.

JENNA. Started telling me how long it takes to decompose. Unbelievable.

HARRIET. Mum'd love that.

JENNA. Then she said, "That's probably not what you want to hear right now." I mean god!

HARRIET. Come on. *(They start to leave. Jenna sees Harriet's plastic bag on the stile.)*

JENNA. Don't forget your arse-bag.

HARRIET. How long does it take? To decompose.

JENNA. Six weeks or so.

HARRIET. Length of the school holidays.

JENNA. Yeah. *(Fade.)*

Scene 4

The living room. A sluggish Sunday afternoon, late November. Alec brings a small fan heater into the room and sets it down on the coffee table. He picks up the plug attached to the heater and looks at it. He exits briefly, and returns, purposeful, a screwdriver in his hand. He goes to start unscrewing the plug casing, then stops. He catches the record player out of the corner of his eye. He goes over to the record player and takes out a record from beneath it. He gently slides it out of its sleeve and blows it to remove any dust. He places the record on the turntable, then bends down to position the needle. Brahms' "Hungarian Dances" plays loudly, then quieter as Alec turns down the volume, a little self-conscious. He holds up the inner sleeve of the record, looking at the light through the translucent circle of plastic in the centre. Alec looks at the fan heater again, then sits down in his armchair and closes his eyes. Harriet enters, a cardboard box in her hand. Alec starts when she comes in and sits up.

HARRIET. Your fridge is where food goes to die. *(Harriet brings the box into the room and puts it on the floor in front of the coffee table. She sits down next to the box with an air of efficiency.)* You know there's things in there went off five years ago? I found a jar of mint jelly right at the back, expired December 1990.
ALEC. Probably still alright …
HARRIET. There's a whole new ecosystem starting in there.
ALEC. So not dying.
HARRIET. What? *(Alec stands up to turn off the record.)*
ALEC. You said food goes there to die. Starting a new ecosystem isn't dying.
HARRIET. Regenerating, then. You don't have to — *[turn the music off.]* *(He lifts the needle off the record anyway.)* Well I've chucked it all so at least no one's dying of botulism. *(Beat.)*
ALEC. What's in the box?
HARRIET. Spices cupboard. It's like an archaeological dig.
ALEC. Does your mother know / about this?
HARRIET. No. Stealth cleaning.
ALEC. She still asleep?
HARRIET. Off and on. 'Least she's resting. I should head home once she's up. *(Alec sits in his chair with the fan heater on the floor and the plug on his lap.)* I used to worry about botulism every time we had spaghetti on toast, you know.
ALEC. Did you?
HARRIET. Dented tins. I really don't mind you having music on …
ALEC. Thought you were in the kitchen.
HARRIET. Felt like some company. *(Alec grimaces.)*
ALEC. You were cold.
HARRIET. It's freezing in there, Dad.

ALEC. I know.

HARRIET. The freezer's got more ice on the outside than — You should get a heater in there. *(Alec points at the heater on the table.)* Oh, OK.

ALEC. Can't get the bloody thing to work. Think it's the fuse. In the plug.

HARRIET. Chuck it out, get a new one. They don't cost much.

ALEC. Might as well try fixing it …

HARRIET. You're so post-war, Dad.

ALEC. Which one?

HARRIET. Crimean. When are they fixing the boiler?

ALEC. Last Thursday. *(Harriet looks at him.)* They have a very, um, *fluid* relationship with time, these heating people. Our weeks of freezing to death are like five minutes of sunshine on their planet. And it's a new model, which means no one's learned how to fix it yet.

HARRIET. Why did you / buy it?

ALEC. Looked warm in the brochure. *(Beat. Alec struggles to undo one of the screws on the plug.)* Dammit. Goddammit.

HARRIET. You alright?

ALEC. Marvellous. *(As he unscrews.)* It's all going terribly well.

HARRIET. Where's Jen?

ALEC. Out with the boyfriend. Some kind of crisis or other.

HARRIET. She showing any sign of moving back into her flat or is she staying here forever now?

ALEC. Daren't ask. *(Myra enters, wearing a dressing gown. She hovers by the door.)*

MYRA. Hi.

ALEC. Sorry, did I wake you?

MYRA. Bloody pipes banging woke me. "Marry a chartered surveyor," they said, "least your house'll always be sound." *(Beat.)* Have you seen upstairs?

HARRIET. Why?

MYRA. All the doors are open. *(Alec and Harriet look at Myra.)* We keep the doors shut up there, don't we? We keep them shut or Baggins gets in and drops hairs all over. On the beds and everything. We're behaving like a family without a cat. Like a non-cat family. He's only been gone a few weeks.

HARRIET. Must've been Jenna.

MYRA. It's not always Jenna. *(Beat. Myra tightens her dressing gown around her.)*

HARRIET. How you feeling?

MYRA. Achy.

HARRIET. Can I get you / anything?

MYRA. No. Thanks. I'm OK.

ALEC. You warm enough?

MYRA. I'm fine. God's sake. *(Myra goes into the kitchen. Harriet watches her. Alec goes back to unscrewing the plug.)*

ALEC. Always cross when she wakes up.

HARRIET. Did you do the doors?

ALEC. Can't remember.

HARRIET. I haven't been upstairs. Apart from seeing Mum. *(Myra returns.)*

MYRA. You've thrown away all the food.

HARRIET. Only the stuff that's gone out of date.

MYRA. It was fine, you don't have to religiously —

HARRIET. Mum, there was mint jelly from 1990.

MYRA. That was fine.

HARRIET. I'd have been fifteen. In 1990. Probably me picked it up in the supermarket. Probably picked up mint jelly instead of mint sauce and that's why it stayed there all this / time.

MYRA. Exactly. There were memories in there.

HARRIET. There was bacteria in there.

MYRA. Beautiful. Circle of life. *(Myra sighs and sits on the sofa. She tucks her legs up under her, painfully.)* Ow ow ow ow ow. *(The others look at her.)* Fine.

ALEC. Permission to give you a blanket?

MYRA. Bugger off. *(Myra points to the box in front of Harriet.)* What's this?

HARRIET. Spice cupboard.

MYRA. Why?

HARRIET. You were asleep. Wanted to do something helpful.

MYRA. You could help me choose a reading for the funeral.

HARRIET. We can go through these together. If you like. *(Alec fumbles and drops part of the plug casing.)*

ALEC. Dammit.

MYRA. What are you doing? *(Alec leans down the side of his seat to pick up the part he's dropped.)*

ALEC. Fixing the heater, for the kitchen.

MYRA. Oh good, that's going to work.

ALEC. What's the matter with you?

MYRA. Cancer. Next question? *(Alec gets up and picks up the heater.)*

ALEC. I did know that. Do this somewhere else. *(Alec goes out to the kitchen.)*

MYRA. Careful, it's cold in there. *(Myra turns back to Harriet.)* Go on, then.

HARRIET. OK. *(Harriet takes out a jar of spice.)* OK. Turmeric. April 2002.

MYRA. Keep that.

HARRIET. Three years.

MYRA. I'll hardly have opened it, there's no air in there.

HARRIET. Right. Tell you what — we'll do a keeping pile and a throwing pile, and if the keeping pile looks too big at the end we'll thin it out, alright?

MYRA. Fine. *(Harriet puts the turmeric to one side.)*

HARRIET. So this is the keeping pile. And rules: We chuck anything over three years old, OK?

MYRA. Great. *(Harriet takes out another jar.)*

HARRIET. Cayenne pepper. August 1998.

MYRA. There was something I used to make with that, what was it?

HARRIET. We're chucking it. Throwing-out pile. *(Harriet puts the cayenne at a distance from the turmeric. Picks out another jar.)* Herbes de Provence.

MYRA. Oh, we should go to Provence again.

HARRIET. 1993. *(Harriet puts the jar with the cayenne on the throwing-out pile. Myra looks at the pile, wistful. Harriet picks out another jar.)* Basil. My god, 2003.

MYRA. Oh goody I can keep it. *(Harriet puts the basil on the keeping pile and goes to pick out another jar.)*

HARRIET. Dad was being nice. Cumin. 1989. *(Myra holds out her hand for the jar.)*

MYRA. Let me see. *(Harriet hands it to her.)* Never used these. *(Myra hands the jar back.)* I know he was being nice.

HARRIET. Chuck?

MYRA. Yes. *(Harriet takes out another.)*

HARRIET. 1991. *(She puts it straight on the throwing-away pile. She will look at several and consign them immediately to the throwing-away pile before she next consults Myra.)* Ask him back in?

MYRA. Harriet, you can't / keep —

HARRIET. I just think —

MYRA. I'm grumpy and tired. And sick. Let me be grumpy today. *(Harriet turns back to the box.)* Jenna lets me be grumpy.

HARRIET. Jenna wouldn't notice if you lost a limb. *(Beat. Harriet takes out another jar.)* Paprika. '95.

MYRA. Mum used to use that. Used to sprinkle it on top of macaroni cheese. She always said paprika was great 'cause it was colourful but didn't really taste of anything. 'Course the answer was it didn't taste of anything in our house 'cause she'd had the jar so long.

HARRIET. You never told me that.

MYRA. Just dust now, isn't it. Chuck it. Chuck all of them, I'm not doing any more cooking.

HARRIET. Don't say that.

MYRA. It's true.

HARRIET. We'll do this another time. *(Harriet starts to hurriedly put all the jars back in the box. Even the throwing-out pile.)*

MYRA. You could just put a sticker or something on all the bad ones and get rid of them when I'm —

HARRIET. We'll do it another time, I've got to get home. *(Harriet finishes putting the jars in the box.)* Do it later. *(Harriet picks up the box, and without looking at Myra, exits to the kitchen. Myra sighs and stands up.)*

MYRA. Ow ow ow ow ow. *(She looks around her, not sure what to do. She sees that Alec's record is still spinning on the turntable and goes over to look at it. She looks at the label in the centre, recognises it and exhales. She stops the record spinning and closes the lid of the player. Alec comes to the doorway with the heater in his arms. He is hesitant.)*

ALEC. I can't find anywhere I'm not snapped at … *(Myra smiles at him gently.)* Is it safe to come out again?

MYRA. Yes, it's safe. *(Alec comes into the room.)*

ALEC. Got it mended, I think.

MYRA. Well done. *(Alec sets the heater down on the table.)*

ALEC. Just plug it in … *(Alec goes over to the socket and inserts the plug. He looks at Myra.)* Cross your fingers. *(Myra holds up her fingers, already crossed, to show him. He moves closer to her and the heater.)*

MYRA. Am I horrible?

ALEC. You're ill. *(Myra squeezes Alec's arm, just above the elbow.)* Here goes. *(Alec reaches out to switch the heater on. They wait for a moment. Nothing happens.)* Little light's supposed to … Check the plug's in properly. *(He goes over to the plug and pushes it harder into the socket. He turns back to Myra, who puts her hand out to feel if anything's coming out of the heater.)* Hot or cold?

MYRA. Nothing. *(She's not sure for a second.)* Hang on … No, nothing. *(Fade.)*

Scene 5

A civil cemetery in Coventry, a dry but cold day in early December. The cemetery has cordoned off a small corner of its land as a vague gesture to the natural burial movement. No one has yet been buried here and it's not difficult to see why — the cemetery is rundown and grim, surrounded by industrial buildings. The natural burial site is little more than a patch of earth. Alec sits on a park bench, the Independent *crossword on his lap. Jenna stands facing him, a tissue in her hand.*

ALEC. Didn't you get the message?

JENNA. What message?

ALEC. Sorry, I left a message on your mobile phone. *(Jenna rummages in her handbag and pulls out her mobile.)*

JENNA. God. Sorry. Don't always hear it in here. *(She sees a message on the phone.)* Um. What did it say?

ALEC. That it'd be me and not your mother. *(Alec rubs his eyes under his glasses.)* She's not brilliant today. *(Jenna twists the tissue in her hands.)*

JENNA. Worse than this morning?

ALEC. Went back to bed about ten. Shouldn't stay out too long. *(Jenna sits down at the other end of the bench from Alec.)*

JENNA. Hello Dad.

ALEC. Hello. *(Alec stands up to take off his coat. He folds it and carefully places it beside him on the bench.)*

JENNA. You hot?

ALEC. No, just a bit —

JENNA. Could they do better for her in the hospital? Maybe if we bullied her together …

ALEC. I don't know, love. It's up to her, isn't it? *(Jenna looks around her.)*

JENNA. This is horrible. This is the worst —

ALEC. Why are we looking at it?

JENNA. It's the closest. On the map — My flat, your house, Harri's house. Nearest there is to equidistant. Mum thinks we'll visit more if we're close by.

ALEC. Shall we go, then?

JENNA. Can we just — I promised we'd give each place a chance, give it a few minutes at least, not dismiss anything. Out of hand. She said you can't always tell just by looking.

ALEC. Well it's warmer than the house. Everywhere's warmer than the house. *(Alec goes back to his crossword. Jenna looks around at the burial ground.)*

JENNA. Is it funereal or funereal? *[fun-er-real or funereal]*

ALEC. *(Without looking up.)* Funereal. *[Funereal]*

JENNA. Always say that wrong. Like ethereal. *[eth-er-real]*

ALEC. Ethereal. *[Ethereal]*

JENNA. Yeah. *(Beat.)* We'll go in a minute.

ALEC. Alright. *(Pause. Alec looks up from his paper, has a vague idea he should say something.)*

JENNA. I saw five separate people fall over in the street today.

ALEC. Did you?

JENNA. Three of them just walking down the street, not massive arse over whatsit falling, just like when your ankle turns and you feel really stupid and you have to do a face ... Then another two on the bus. I was on the bus, they were on the pavement. Started to wonder if it was me making them fall just by looking at them, like the tree falling down in a wood thing, but I tried it on lots of other people and they didn't fall over and then I got here. Do you miss her?

ALEC. Miss her?

JENNA. Like when people say "missing you already." I miss her already sometimes. It — *(Alec frowns.)* Have you got anything to eat?

ALEC. No.

JENNA. Haven't had any lunch.

ALEC. Oh, hang on. *(Alec feels in his pocket and pulls out a Fry's Peppermint Cream chocolate bar. He hands it to Jenna.)*

JENNA. Ooh, your favourite!

ALEC. Don't tell your mother.

JENNA. I hide chocolate too. *(Jenna opens the packet. She takes a piece and eats it.)* Had these when you were little, didn't you? What was the other one?

ALEC. Five Boys. Fry's Five Boys chocolate.

JENNA. What was that like?

ALEC. Chocolate with a picture of five boys on the top. *(Jenna eats another piece of chocolate.)*

31

JENNA. D'you want some?

ALEC. No thanks love, you have it.

JENNA. Got some more in the car?

ALEC. No. *(Alec goes back to his crossword. Jenna finishes the bar of chocolate in silence.)*

JENNA. Can I put your coat on?

ALEC. If you want. *(Jenna stands up and puts the coat on over the top of her jacket. She sits down, her arms hugging the coat around her.)*

JENNA. It's really cold here.

ALEC. We can go.

JENNA. In a minute. *(Alec looks up. Tries to make conversation.)*

ALEC. Where's Martin today?

JENNA. Mark.

ALEC. Mark.

JENNA. Think he wants to split up. *(Beat. Alec looks away, tired.)*

ALEC. Does he?

JENNA. Think you were right not liking him. *(Pause. Alec rubs his eyes.)*

ALEC. I'm sorry, I —

JENNA. No, dads aren't supposed to like the boyfriend, are they? Just isn't nice to me anymore. Since he started this stupid course. Just — just wants to be with his stupid college friends. Some of them are, like, barely twenty and he's over thirty — it's pathetic. Tells me he doesn't have enough money when I suggest we go out to eat, or go out or whatever, but he's got enough money to go to the pub after every class and —

ALEC. Maybe you just … you've just … Hmm. *(Jenna frowns. Alec looks at the sky.)*

JENNA. Like last week I finally persuaded him to let me meet his stupid new friends, this is after weeks of saying, "Why don't I come and meet you after college," and him saying, "No, you're alright" and changing the subject and me thinking, "Oh for fuck's sake!" Sorry.

ALEC. It's all / right.

JENNA. So, I go to meet him after a seminar and talk to his friends and I thought I'd been OK, just myself, thought I made quite a good impression, you know? And then we got back to his, and he said I'd *embarrassed* him and I'd *monopolised* the conversation …

ALEC. You can get a bit …

JENNA. I feel like we're already splitting up, like I can feel it beginning to end. Sometimes I can hear the end of it in his voice.

And I get so worried about Mum and stuff, you know? I need someone *there*. And then he says I'm clingy, I'm too needy. And I'm like, "What d'you expect, my mum's got cancer … " *(Pause. Alec searches for something to say.)*
ALEC. He's probably just … Hmm.
JENNA. We don't even have sex anymore …
ALEC. You don't have to / tell me about that.
JENNA. Sorry. *(Beat.)*
ALEC. I can't really do … problems.
JENNA. No, sorry. *(Beat. She puts her head on his shoulder. He flinches, almost imperceptibly.)*
ALEC. I've got to get back. *(Alec stands up.)* D'you want a lift? *(Jenna looks at him, then down at the ground.)*
JENNA. Yes please.
ALEC. I'll bring the car 'round. *(Alec walks off to the car park. Jenna is left watching him go. She pulls the coat around her, tightly, and looks at the cemetery, twisting her tissue. Fade.)*

Scene 6

The living room, Friday evening, late January. Jenna and Harriet sit on the sofa, their hands on their laps, silent, preoccupied, their faces disordered. Both have the slightly inflated look of wearing several layers of clothing and each has more than one scarf around her neck. They are both staring at a white cardboard coffin, on the carpet in front of them. Long pause.

JENNA. So that's it, then.
HARRIET. Yes. *(Pause.)*
JENNA. That's it.
HARRIET. Yes. *(Pause.)*
JENNA. That's what it looks like.
HARRIET. Yes. *(Pause.)*
JENNA. Looks big.
HARRIET. Sometimes fat people die. *(Jenna laughs, then stops herself.)*
JENNA. Wasn't very hard, was it?
HARRIET. Like IKEA.

JENNA. Funny they haven't changed the shape. Hundreds of years and they still look like that. Still looks like a coffin. *(Jenna stands up and goes to the coffin. She takes the lid off.)* Need some cushions, make it nice in there. *(She touches the plastic lining of the coffin. It crackles.)* Know what this is?

HARRIET. What?

JENNA. Cremfilm.

HARRIET. Nice.

JENNA. Fluids.

HARRIET. Yeah. *(Jenna crackles it again.)*

JENNA. Think we'll get something else. Feels a bit freezer bag. *(Jenna runs her fingers along the side of the coffin.)*

HARRIET. Does it feel strong?

JENNA. Yeah. We should start painting.

HARRIET. Should draw it on first. With pencil.

JENNA. Shall I fetch her, show it to her?

HARRIET. D'you want to? *(They consider it.)* Show her later. Once we've done some drawing.

JENNA. OK.

HARRIET. Sky and stars.

JENNA. I'm shit at art.

HARRIET. Me too.

JENNA. You're not shit at anything.

HARRIET. I'll get pencils. *(Harriet goes to the kitchen. Jenna looks at the coffin, biting her thumbnail. Alec enters, holding a telephone and a piece of paper. He stops and looks at the coffin. Jenna holds her hands out towards it, presenting it, an awkward magician.)*

JENNA. Ta-dah! *(Pause.)*

ALEC. That's it then.

JENNA. Yeah. *(Pause.)*

ALEC. Good. Good Lord. *(Alec looks around the room, anywhere but the coffin.)* I'm looking for my — Ah. *(He sees his pullover on his armchair.)* There we are. *(He picks up the pullover to wear over the top of the one he's wearing already. He pulls it on sleeves first, then head. He looks at the phone.)* Right. *(He starts to tap in a number, from the piece of paper in his hand.)*

JENNA. Who you ringing?

ALEC. Boiler people. Give them a piece of my mind.

JENNA. Good luck. *(Alec finishes tapping in the number and listens to it ringing. Harriet returns with two pencils.)*

HARRIET. Sorry, lots of crap in the pencil drawer. *(She hands one*

to Jenna and looks enquiringly at Alec.)
ALEC. On hold.
JENNA. Boiler firm.
ALEC. Vivaldi. "Spring."
HARRIET. Brilliant. *(Alec tries to stay turned away from the coffin but keeps catching it out of the corner of his eye. Jenna watches him.)* So what we doing?
JENNA. *(Points to the feet end of the coffin.)* Sky. *(And to the head end.)* Stars.
HARRIET. That way 'round?
JENNA. Don't want stars 'round her feet, do we?
HARRIET. So she's what, standing on a cloud? Just get her a harp and be done with it …
JENNA. What she asked for.
HARRIET. So clouds down here, stars up here …
ALEC. Is that what she wants on it, clouds and stars?
JENNA. Something like that. *(Alec stares at the coffin. He starts as someone answers the phone.)*
ALEC. Oh, um, sorry — Sorry, can I — Can I call you back? *(He hangs up, quickly. Sees the others watching him.)* Do it later. Have to be in the right mood. *(Harriet and Jenna turn back to the coffin. Alec edges towards it.)* So how much did it — How much did it cost, this?
JENNA. 'Bout seventy pounds.
ALEC. Well. Bargain.
HARRIET. I'll start on the sky, yeah? Think I can do clouds.
JENNA. I'll do stars. *(Harriet and Jenna tentatively start to draw on the coffin.)*
ALEC. Is that what they — Do they all cost that?
JENNA. Approximately. Not a very competitive market.
ALEC. Does a more. Expensive one look. Look less like a cardboard box?
JENNA. Won't look like a box when it's painted.
ALEC. Doesn't look strong enough.
JENNA. We're not the first people to ever use one.
ALEC. No.
JENNA. We could test it.
ALEC. No, I don't think so. *(Alec paces around the coffin.)* What's that inside it?
JENNA. Cremfilm.
ALEC. For the, um —
JENNA. Fluids.

ALEC. Right. *(Alec looks out of the window.)* Right. *(Harriet and Jenna look at each other. An awkward pause.)*

HARRIET. I've got a new game, Dad.

ALEC. Have you, love?

HARRIET. Josh thought of it. We were taking about cocoa farmers. *(Jenna sniggers.)* Shut up. About what a shitty time they have and stuff, and then Josh says he's never seen a cocoa bean. Which is stupid because he's been everywhere. Like he doesn't know what one looks like, he just knows the word, knows what they are. So we started a game of thinking of things you've never seen.

ALEC. Hmm.

HARRIET. D'you know what I mean? Not like an elephant because you might not actually have *seen* an elephant but you know what it looks like 'cause you've seen pictures — something you have no idea what it looks like but you know the word for.

ALEC. A competent boiler engineer. D'you see the one they sent last week? Must've been about fourteen. Promise they're sending 'round someone decent, someone with half a whatsit, then you open the door and you can tell straight off. Different monkey, same zoo … Good game. *(Short pause.)*

JENNA. Don't think I've ever seen a carburettor.

ALEC. You must / have.

JENNA. No, I haven't, I'm sure I haven't.

HARRIET. Isn't that the bit, the bit attached to the / exhaust pipe?

ALEC. Exhaust pipe. The wider bit.

JENNA. Is it? Oh, I've seen that, is that what it is?

ALEC. Yes.

JENNA. OK. *(Pause. They think.)* I've never seen a slide rule.

HARRIET. Oh, good one.

JENNA. No mental picture.

ALEC. It's like a — I've got one, actually.

JENNA. See, I didn't even know it was small enough to go in a house.

ALEC. Upstairs somewhere. I could dig it out. I'll go and —

JENNA. Dad, it's / OK.

ALEC. In the study I think. *(Alec leaves.)*

HARRIET. Go and have a look.

JENNA. We're doing this.

HARRIET. Make him happy, he likes showing things.

JENNA. He'll bring it down if he finds it. *(They continue to draw.)* Is this how it'll be, d'you think? The three of us.

HARRIET. Don't know. *(Beat.)*

JENNA. What was your thing?

HARRIET. What?

JENNA. Thing you'd never seen.

HARRIET. Oh. Big one. Never seen a dead body. *(Pause. Jenna thinks.)*

JENNA. Yeah, but that doesn't fit, does it? With the game. You know what that's going to look like. It'll look like Mum. *(Harriet puts down her pencil.)*

HARRIET. These clouds look like turds. *(Jenna looks.)* I'd have learned to draw properly, you know, if I'd known … *(They examine their work so far.)*

JENNA. You know what Baggins'd do? He'd get in there, curl up and have a sleep. Loved boxes.

HARRIET. "My cat likes to hide in boxes."

JENNA. Wouldn't even be bothered what it's for. *(They look at the coffin, then at each other.)*

HARRIET. You.

JENNA. No, you.

HARRIET. You.

JENNA. You're the oldest.

HARRIET. You're the naughtiest.

JENNA. You won't be cross?

HARRIET. Why would I be cross?

JENNA. You know, all self-righteous like, "Ooh, you shouldn't have done that."

HARRIET. No.

JENNA. OK. *(Jenna steps gingerly into the coffin. She sits down, pulling her knees up under her chin. Harriet watches her, intently.)*

HARRIET. Lie down.

JENNA. Might snag the Cremfilm.

HARRIET. Go on. *(Jenna looks at Harriet, then lies down slowly.)* How is it?

JENNA. Twenty years ago you'd have put the lid on and sat on it. *(Beat.)* Never looked at this ceiling before, looks fucking awful. Look at that crack. *(Jenna's hand comes up out of the coffin, pointing.)* Place is falling to bits. *(Harriet hears a noise, off. Jenna sits up and looks around.)*

HARRIET. Coming downstairs. *(Jenna clambers hastily out of the coffin. They look at each other.)*

JENNA. This didn't happen. We didn't do this.

HARRIET. No, that'd be —

JENNA. Wrong. Morbid. *(Alec returns, shaking his head.)*

ALEC. Couldn't find it. Buried under years of crap.

HARRIET. Another time.

ALEC. Your mother's coming down, she's woken up.

HARRIET. Right. Great. *(Alec paces, rattling the change in his pockets. Jenna shivers.)*

ALEC. You're not going to do anything —

JENNA. What?

ALEC. Alarming.

JENNA. Not about me, is it? *(Myra comes in, rubbing sleep from her eyes, slightly dopey. The others all look at her.)*

MYRA. Let me see it. *(The others move away so that Myra has a clear view of the coffin. Myra looks at it. She wakes up. Looks at it for a long time.)* That's it, then. *(Pause.)* Was it difficult?

HARRIET. Instructions were good, very clear.

JENNA. You need them clear, don't you, I mean it's a difficult time, you don't want to be ... *(Myra continues to look at the coffin without moving towards it.)* It'll look better once it's painted. Once Harriet learns to draw clouds.

MYRA. Thought I was painting it.

JENNA. Well, if that's what you — I just thought —

MYRA. I'll paint it. *(Myra frowns.)* Doesn't look how I thought.

JENNA. It's good and strong.

ALEC. What did you expect, a Wendy house?

MYRA. Doesn't look very wide.

JENNA. It's wider than you, we measured when we ordered it. *(Pause.)*

MYRA. I think I'd like to be buried on my side.

HARRIET. On your side?

MYRA. Like the way I sleep. On my side. With my legs tucked up. My hands under my / face. *(Myra mimes where her hands would go.)*

ALEC. Oh for God's / sake!

MYRA. So it's like going to sleep. What?

ALEC. Just rewrite the whole bloody —

MYRA. I just think I'd be less. Less scared of the earth.

ALEC. You won't be conscious.

MYRA. All that earth coming down. On top of me.

ALEC. It doesn't make any / difference ...

MYRA. Wouldn't you be scared? *(Beat. She looks at the three of them.)* D'you know what I read today? Something I never knew.

38

Never knew before. When you die, if you've eaten, if you've got any food in in your system, in your *bowels*, horrible word — When you die, all your muscles relax. Including your, your rectum. So if there's. If there's anything *there* when you die, next thing you do is, um, is shit. After you die, you can shit. I might die while you're all out of the house and you might come home and find me covered in — Your last picture of me. I won't, you're right, Alec, I won't know about it. Still can't bear it. *(The others watch her, paralysed. Myra looks at her family.)* Look at you. Will one of you please for a bloody change know what to do? *(Pause. Harriet goes to Myra and puts her arms around her. Myra looks at Alec over Harriet's shoulder. Fade.)*

Scene 7

A burial ground in Coventry. Wednesday afternoon, the kind of surprisingly warm mid-March day that provokes premature summer behaviour. This is a mature woodland which has only recently been converted into a burial site. Graves are placed between the trees, with no markers except for a small plaque on a tree close to each grave. The ground under the trees is carpeted with moss and there are daffodils and crocuses. Jenna sits under a tree, looking around her, smoking. Harriet enters, a little dishevelled. Jenna looks up and sees her.

JENNA. Oh, for fuck's sake.
HARRIET. What?
JENNA. It's supposed to be Mum. Does she have to keep sending proxies? I know what she's doing, I'm not a fucking social cripple and my phone's been on all morning 'cause I checked it, before you start. *(Harriet looks at the back of her hands.)*
HARRIET. Said she's fed up of us coming home saying they're not right. Says she doesn't need to see them if they're all going to be not right.
JENNA. But I think this one might be.
HARRIET. Really?
JENNA. Yeah. *(Harriet looks around her.)*
HARRIET. Yeah. Proper wood.

JENNA. Be gorgeous in summer. The crocuses are nice.

HARRIET. Croci. *[Croaky]*

JENNA. *(In a croaky voice.)* The crocuses are nice.

HARRIET. Oh, funny. *(Jenna has to cough to clear her throat.)*

JENNA. 'Scuse me. I bet there's bluebells. I bet it's all covered in bluebells in the summer. *(Beat.)*

HARRIET. I don't want it to be summer.

JENNA. How d'you mean?

HARRIET. When she dies. Winter's easier, everyone's all bundled up, rushing around busy and no one has to ask you, you don't get *asked* ... Summer you're supposed to be happy, aren't you? People being happy all over the place, it's all warm, you. Can't wear your scarf anymore. Couples all over the place, all being new with each other, all happy and *new* ...

JENNA. You alright? *(Harriet looks at Jenna, then away.)*

HARRIET. No. No, I'm losing it. Quite successfully. *(Harriet looks at Jenna, smiles weakly.)* Doesn't matter. It's not about me.

JENNA. How losing it? *(Harriet scratches the backs of her hands as she speaks.)*

HARRIET. Just — Not being able to — Feels like — I don't know, you know how sometimes you're doing laundry and you'll — You take it all out the machine and for some reason you've left the basket somewhere else so you have to carry it all up the stairs in your arms and —

JENNA. I haven't got stairs.

HARRIET. What?

JENNA. Moved out of Mum's yesterday.

HARRIET. Oh. Really? Wow. Really?

JENNA. Back in my flat now.

HARRIET. OK.

JENNA. Laundry.

HARRIET. Yeah. So I'm trying to carry it all up the stairs. And. And it's quite a big pile and I can't see where my feet are on the steps 'cause it's so big so I'm slow ... But then one sock falls off the top of the pile and I bend down to pick it up but while I'm doing that something else falls and I can't pick each thing up without dropping something else and then. Before I know it I've tripped up a step and there's washing all over the floor. Except it's not wash-ing, it's me all over the floor. But hey ho. *(Harriet smiles sadly and shakes her head.)* And I've got this stupid eczema or something — never had eczema — backs of my hands keep itching all the time

... Are the graves under the trees?

JENNA. Spaces between. Trees are too old, aren't they?

HARRIET. Oh yeah.

JENNA. Little marker on each one to say who's there, look. *(She twists 'round to look at the tree behind her.)* ... Dorothy Hutchins. Must have been old, don't get kids called Dorothy, do you? Hope there's no babies ... E45 cream. Stop it itching. *(Harriet paces, animated, slightly off-balance.)*

HARRIET. You know, I went to mum's the other day, just to check up on her and stuff. Walked in and she's sat in the coffin. Middle of the living room floor and she's — She's watching *Have I Got News For You* and she's laughing. Sitting in it, laughing. And I just thought god, I can't cope with this I can't do this. I was looking at her and I missed her. Don't know what I'm going to do. It hurts behind my eyes. Got this stupid eczema. My mouth keeps tasting of blood and it's not bleeding gums 'cause I thought it must be and I went to the dentist. *(Harriet stares into the distance, her hand to her mouth.)*

JENNA. I've got Tic-Tacs.

HARRIET. Yeah?

JENNA. Want one?

HARRIET. Please. *(Jenna pulls a box of Tic-Tacs out of her bag and holds them out. Harriet goes to her and takes the box.)*

JENNA. Have two if you like. Should carry Tic-Tacs. Or gum. Minty stuff's good, it makes you concentrate on it, you stop thinking about whatever you're thinking about and start thinking of. Mint. *(Harriet takes two and hands the box back.)*

HARRIET. Thanks.

JENNA. Better? *(Harriet paces again.)*

HARRIET. Yeah. I keep — I can't — Can't stop *feeling*. Can't get on with my life because I'm *feeling* all the time. Can't do anything. Keep crying. Or thinking I'm going to cry and then not being able to do anything in case I do. Josh thinks I need to *(Imitating his voice.)* "go and talk to someone." Which just makes me think, "What the fuck are you there for, then?"

JENNA. Are you going to? Talk to someone.

HARRIET. Don't know. Usually I'd talk to / Mum.

JENNA. Mum. Yeah. *(Beat.)*

HARRIET. Think I'll sit down now.

JENNA. You'll get a wet arse. *(Harriet sits next to Jenna.)* You could talk to me. If you want to. I mean, I won't be upset if you — Know I'm less use than a snot rag in most. Situations. But. You know ...

HARRIET. Yeah.

JENNA. Everyone thinks I'm mad as a bucket, complete liability but — Not always.

HARRIET. Thanks. *(Beat.)*

JENNA. I finished with Mark.

HARRIET. You?

JENNA. Yup.

HARRIET. Why?

JENNA. Just — It's really boring. Just I realised I didn't want him at the funeral. Then I thought about it some more and I realised I didn't want *him.*

HARRIET. God. How are you?

JENNA. Oh, you know. Miss him.

HARRIET. When was this?

JENNA. Last week. Week ago.

HARRIET. What's Mum think?

JENNA. Haven't told her. Didn't tell anyone. *(Harriet looks at her.)* Thought I should have a practice. *(Jenna takes out her Tic Tacs and eats one. Pause. Harriet stands up.)*

HARRIET. I've got a wet arse.

JENNA. That's awful, isn't it? Practising.

HARRIET. No, it — *(Pause. Jenna looks at the floor.)*

JENNA. The moss is nice. I like the moss.

HARRIET. Yeah. Furry.

JENNA. Warm. Like a blanket. *(Beat.)*

HARRIET. I need to go.

JENNA. OK. *(Beat. Harriet looks around.)*

HARRIET. Yeah.

JENNA. OK. *(Jenna stands up for the first time, revealing the plastic bag she's been sitting on. She folds it up carefully and puts it into her handbag. Harriet watches her, surprised. Jenna looks up and sees Harriet watching.)* What? *(Harriet laughs.)* What? *(Fade.)*

Scene 8

The living room, early evening, mid-March. Myra's card-board coffin, now half-painted with sky and stars, is at the side of the sofa, its lid lying beside it. Alec has the phone in his hand and is pacing up and down. He has a letter in his hand, which he refers to occasionally.

ALEC. The reference number at the *bottom* of the page? ... LS23161701 ... Mr. A. Bradley, 26 Morris Avenue, look you know who I am, we've been on the phone all bloody week ... Right. I've got a letter in my hand saying you were going to come 'round today and sort it out ... Oh yes, someone came, someone came and scratched his head at it, had a cup of tea, said he couldn't fix it and toddled off again. Which to be honest isn't what I had in mind. Listen, mate — I'm sorry, do you mind if I call you mate, it's not a word I'd normally use, but I feel we've spent a lot of time together now ... Richard. Right. Richard. Richard, when are you going to fix my boiler? ... Alright, try again: When — *specifically,* in *time* — are you going to fix my boiler? ... Mmm, uh-huh ... Do you know I have never encountered incompetence on this level before? My daughter has this thing she says (she's twenty-seven, she talks like a teenager) the thing she keeps saying is "next-level," everything's next-level wrong, next-level horrid, next-level stupid. Well this is next-level farcical if that's not a tautology ... *Tautology.* It means — It doesn't matter ... Could you just — Could you *let* me complain at you, I'm afraid I won't feel complete until I've ruined your day too. I mean what is the *point,* what is the blasted point of making a boiler so high-tech there's only two chaps in the country can fix it? What is the bloody point? ... So if you agree, why can't you do something about it? Somebody somewhere in your company has to take responsibility — How many people where you're working, Richard? ... How many can you see? ... Where are you? ... Good god, no wonder you don't care about my problems if you're in *Glasgow.* Right, so I'm imagining, if the world's a fair place, that the others are spending a good portion of their time being screamed at by someone like me, I mean, I can't believe I'm completely alone in this … So what if you get everyone together and count up the amount of time you've spent listening to complaints about the CH-2010, which incidentally isn't the year you're going to fix my boiler in, and then you might work out there's a health and safety issue, something about stress and eardrums and you can all take your headpieces off and go over and tell the supervisor and maybe if you all club together and do something about it you might have the — Hmm. *(Alec stops. He takes his glasses off and rubs his eyes.)* No, that's crap. Don't have the power to do anything, do you? *(Alec paces around the coffin, looking at it.)* We've been cold for four months. You know how cold a house gets after that long? Nothing residual left.

Tell you something else — my wife is dying … No — no, it's not your fault … Cancer. Bone cancer … No, she's going to die. So you can imagine how this is making me weary. I am spending precious hours of her dwindling life talking to you. She wants to stay at home, she doesn't want to die in hospital, she wants to die at home, which between you and me I think is a drastically bad idea, but that's what she wants and by Christ I'll get it for her if I have to come to Glasgow and do the bloody training course myself … No, I'm a. I'm a chartered surveyor … No, we don't do heating systems … Look, what it boils down to, excuse the pun, in essence what I'm saying here is the least you can do is let her die in the *warm*. It's bafflingly little to ask. *(Alec stands in the coffin.)* … When? … DID YOU NOT HEAR A WORD I SAID? I want someone out here tomorrow, Richard. Tomorrow morning. *(Myra enters carrying a pot of silver paint, which she stirs with a small paintbrush. She is wearing her dressing gown.)* … Yes, Thursday should be fine. Yes, two o'clock. *(Alec hangs up the phone. He takes a breath.)* Thursday.

MYRA. I heard.

ALEC. House is falling apart.

MYRA. You could move. *(Alec steps out of the coffin and moves away.)*

ALEC. The walls are bowing. *(Myra laughs.)*

MYRA. It's aching. Heaving, like when you cry. Like when a person who cries, cries.

ALEC. Just years of neglect, love. *(Alec rubs his eyes under his glasses. He sits down in his chair.)* Nice bath? *(Myra eases herself down by the coffin. Alec watches the pain in her movements.)*

MYRA. Alright. Didn't stay in long, too much Radox, got a bit gritty. Going off baths, too much thinking time. *(She starts to add another coat of paint to the silver stars on the coffin.)*

ALEC. You think I should move house?

MYRA. Up to you. *(She paints. Pause.)* Alec, when I'm gone —

ALEC. I don't want to talk about — / I shouldn't have —

MYRA. Something really important I —

ALEC. Sleep on your side, fine, I don't care, do whatever —

MYRA. Not that something else. *(Alec looks at her, confused.)* I have to — Something I have to — You might meet someone else.

ALEC. What?

MYRA. Once I've gone. You might meet someone, you might want to — *(Alec goes to speak. Stopping him:)* No, please don't please don't. *(Continuing.)* You might find you — There might be some part of you that, that *can't*, because you feel I wouldn't — That it'd be ... You might hold back from it, you might not even — and I — I want you to *know* that's not what I want for you. *(Beat.)*

ALEC. Christ, Myra.

MYRA. You just don't know, do you? I mean, she might just turn up one day, just like that, out of the blue. And if she does, when she does, I don't want you to feel you can't — can't say hello. *(Alec shifts in his chair.)* You're not expecting it now, but — Alec, you could fall in love! You could fall so much in love, you could feel something *violent*. And you've got to be brave and and um *go for it* because that's what I want you to do. In that situation. Or even. Even if it's not violent I mean. There's no reason to be alone, you're too young to — *(Alec stands up. He goes over to the window and takes his handkerchief out of his pocket. He wipes his eyes, facing away from Myra. A long pause.)*

ALEC. When did — When did we — When did we stop fighting this and just accept it? *(Myra goes back to painting.)*

MYRA. You know, you should switch to paper hankies. Women don't like those. *(Beat.)*

ALEC. When did we decide you weren't ever — *(Myra continues painting.)* I can't remember that talk, I don't remember us deciding ...

MYRA. You could just say thank you. *(Beat.)* Thank you for arranging everything. Thank you for making sure everything's covered, not — Not forgetting anything, forgetting to say anything. *(Long pause. Alec looks out of the window, composes himself, softens.)*

ALEC. Thank you. *(He tries to find words.)* You know the funeral isn't. Isn't for you. It's for us. Maybe if you could leave us, maybe something to do. To be — To be occupied with. After you — People need something to do. *(Myra sits still. She puts the paintbrush down.)* Something to do. *(Alec goes to his chair and picks up a book from beside it. He is about to sit down, then changes his mind and goes to sit down on one end of the sofa, closer to where Myra is. He opens his book and starts to read.)*

MYRA. I'm sorry. *(Alec looks over the top of his glasses at Myra.)* Thank you for sorting out the boiler. That was —

ALEC. Least I could do. *(Alec looks back at his book. A sad smile breaks Myra's face. She comes closer to Alec and sits next to him. Hesitant, she takes his arm and puts it around her shoulder, leaning her back against his side and pulling her feet up so that she is sitting lengthways on the sofa. She almost daren't breathe in case he notices and shrugs her away. Alec tenses, then relaxes. He continues to read, trying to turn the pages with one hand.)*

MYRA. Look after the girls, won't you? *(Alec looks up.)*

ALEC. Are you —

MYRA. What?

ALEC. All this talk, are you thinking it's tonight or —

MYRA. Oh no. No, weeks left. Lots more awkward talks. *(Pause. Alec goes back to his book.)* When my dad died, mum said she'd woken up sometimes afterwards and felt him in the room. Felt him sit down. On the edge of the bed, an actual weight. A presence. She was awake, she wasn't even — But then I haven't sat on your bed for years, so … *(Alec gives up and closes the book, placing it on the arm of the sofa beside him. He takes off his glasses and places them on top of the book.)* Maybe tonight? *(She leans her head back on his shoulder. Alec plants a gentle kiss on top of Myra's head. Pause.)*

ALEC. You know I — I do um. Cry. I will, when you — You mustn't think I I won't. *(Pause.)*

MYRA. OK. *(Pause.)*

ALEC. Help you upstairs …

MYRA. No, stay here a minute. Liking this. *(Alec puts his other arm around her and holds her tight.)*

ALEC. My room or your room? *(Myra laughs.)*

MYRA. Yours is tidier. *(Fade.)*

Scene 9

The same burial ground as in Scene 7, but now, in late March, the crocuses and daffodils are in full bloom and the morning sunlight is partially obscured by new leaves on the trees. The site has increased in beauty since we last saw it. Myra and Jenna stand surveying the site. Myra is wearing a coat, Jenna isn't. Jenna carries a blanket under her arm.

JENNA. Here?

MYRA. Here.

JENNA. I think so. I think it's —

MYRA. Yes. Yes it is. *(Pause. Jenna looks off.)*

JENNA. Is Harri coming?

MYRA. Said she wanted to stay in the car.

JENNA. OK. *(Jenna takes the blanket and spreads it out on the ground.)* Get you sat down.

MYRA. Can I sit on the moss?

JENNA. Um, I gue— *(She touches the moss with the palm of her hand.)* Yes, it's dry. *(Jenna helps Myra to sit down on the floor. Jenna stands up again and looks at Myra, curious.)*

MYRA. What?

JENNA. You didn't make a noise. When you sat down.

MYRA. Full to my earlobes with painkillers, love.

JENNA. Right.

MYRA. I'm not getting / better —

JENNA. No, I know. *(Pause.)*

MYRA. Should have died last Thursday. If it was six months.

JENNA. But you didn't.

MYRA. Bit busy that day. Postponed it. *(Myra laughs.)* I haven't been counting or anything. Not really, I just. I looked at the dates when they first told me. It's not like they say, "You've got until the twenty-second of March," or something, I just looked at the dates, so — Yes. Think we'll know about it before it happens — all that standing 'round my bed bit to get through yet ... Need to buy a big nightie.

JENNA. I'll get you a big nightie. M&S.

MYRA. Thanks. Anyhow, all of this is extra. All of this is better

47

than expected.

JENNA. Yeah.

MYRA. Except I've been having headaches.

JENNA. Right. Which means —

MYRA. Skull. *(They think.)*

JENNA. Should've brought some sandwiches.

MYRA. I'm sorry, I didn't / think —

JENNA. No, I mean, I should have. Not your job anymore. I mean, I don't mean — I mean I should've thought of it.

MYRA. Should've brought champagne. Celebrate finding this place, it's gorgeous.

JENNA. Yeah.

MYRA. I could be really happy here. Could really be beautiful. *(Beat. Jenna thinks.)*

JENNA. What food d'you want? At the funeral, you know, we haven't talked about — What? *(Myra is laughing.)*

MYRA. I hadn't — I hadn't even thought about — *(Stops herself laughing.)* You choose. I won't have to eat it. Choose something you like.

JENNA. OK. I mean, I might not eat anything, I might not feel like it …

MYRA. I brought something for you … *(Myra looks in her hand-bag and pulls out a business card. She hands it to Jenna.)*

JENNA. Who's this?

MYRA. She was at the hospital. Does green funerals. Like a funeral director, but much more personal, family involved a lot more, that kind of thing. She can arrange everything, you just tell her what you want. I wouldn't mind if you called her.

JENNA. Mum, we can manage it …

MYRA. But you might feel. I don't know. Alone with it. Like the old bitch has died and now you've got to deal with all this paperwork or whatever … You might need someone.

JENNA. I know we've made it look really difficult, but —

MYRA. It's not a criticism. *(Jenna turns away, putting the business card in the back pocket of her trousers.)*

JENNA. I thought of something we could throw in.

MYRA. Oh yes?

JENNA. Instead of flowers or your stupid glitter idea.

MYRA. What?

JENNA. Leaf skeletons. That could be beautiful.

MYRA. Yes.

JENNA. Might kind of. Float. *(Jenna paces. She smiles.)*

MYRA. What is it?

JENNA. Nothing. You warm enough?

MYRA. Toasty. Lovely day. Glad I didn't die in winter. Less chance of the funeral getting rained on now. Couldn't bear it if you all had to carry umbrellas, want you to see each others' faces. Easier to be *open* in summer, isn't it? *(Pause.)*

JENNA. I don't know how open we're going to be, Mum. It doesn't feel — Easy. To learn. I think you want the three of us to have this fully functioning — Talking thing. And I don't know if we will. 'Cause we never have. I used to notice, going to the loo in the middle of the night, I'd be walking down a corridor of closed doors. Like a hotel. Four separate people. That time I moved back in, before Christmas, I tried leaving all the doors open, see if it'd help. I'd go upstairs and open all the doors. And someone else would always go 'round and close them all again. So I don't know if — If we never had that even with you here, I don't know if we'll do it without you. *(Myra strokes the moss on the ground beside her.)* Sorry. *(Jenna sits down beside Myra. She bites her thumbnail. Then she catches sight of something on Myra's skirt.)* Look.

MYRA. What?

JENNA. Cat hair. *(Myra peers at it. Jenna carefully picks it off.)* That's Baggins.

MYRA. Is it?

JENNA. Ginger at the tip and white at the bottom. Definitely him.

MYRA. Shows how long ago I washed it. Miss that cat. *(Beat. They look at the cat hair.)*

JENNA. I'm really sorry.

MYRA. Blow it. Make a wish.

JENNA. That's eyelashes, isn't it?

MYRA. Blow it anyway. *(Jenna does.)* Don't tell me. Hope you get it. *(Myra brushes down her skirt, removing any other hairs.)* I know it's not going to be perfect the three of you but — I know that. God, if you turn into the Waltons the second I'm gone I'll be really cross 'cause I'll just think why couldn't you do that years ago, why couldn't we all enjoy that together? But — You don't know what you can do. Look at you — you left him all by yourself and you survived it and now look at you, you're smiling all over the place …

JENNA. Yeah.

MYRA. I mean I. I think you might be able to manage without me.

JENNA. Oh Mum, I.

MYRA. Which is OK. *(Jenna looks away.)* Tell you something. When I first met your dad, he wouldn't — He wouldn't listen to music if there was anyone else there. Hated it, had to leave the room, wouldn't go to the opera or anything. Get up and turn the record off if you walked in. Hated it if you came in quietly and caught him. Used to drive me up the wall. All this going to concerts business, it's all quite new. Only the last what, fifteen years or so. When Harriet started playing the silly cello, that's when it started. Knew I'd never sit through a whole concerto so he had to do it. But before that, only if he was on his own. *(Beat.)* You'd never have known that.

JENNA. No.

MYRA. So he's come on, you see. Since then. You know, there's always room for — Things are possible. People can — Maybe we shouldn't have Brahms at the funeral. Might be too much.

JENNA. How is he? Is he OK?

MYRA. He's got the boiler fixed. Which is a relief, you know, now the weather's warmer anyway … *(They laugh.)* Now he can get on with worrying about the walls bowing and the roof leaking and the pipes banging and all the rest … And he's going to be fine. Harri's going to be fine in a bit. You're all going to be fine and it's exciting and I won't bloody well be here to see it. *(Beat.)* Time is it?

JENNA. Twelve.

MYRA. Tablet time. *(Myra looks in her handbag.)* Left them in the car.

JENNA. I'll get them. Then we don't have to leave yet.

MYRA. Could you bring the water as well?

JENNA. Sure.

MYRA. And Harri, maybe?

JENNA. Give it a go. *(Jenna is about to go. She sees the blanket.)* Take this thing back if we're not sitting on it. *(She bends down to fold up the blanket. Myra catches her smiling as she does it.)*

MYRA. Is it something specific you're smiling about?

JENNA. Not smiling.

MYRA. It's OK to smile. *(Jenna stands up, the blanket clutched to her.)*

JENNA. OK. New man. *(Myra looks at her, surprised.)* Yeah.

MYRA. Who is he?

JENNA. He's not a wanker.

MYRA. Good lord.

JENNA. He's — God, there's too much to —

MYRA. How's the sex?

JENNA. Amazing. He's so, um — We didn't do it till the fourth night. I've got this — this pulse in my bottom lip all the time. He's just — You need your tablets. *(Jenna goes to leave.)* I'll be quick. Don't go anywhere.

MYRA. Make pretty slow progress if I did.

JENNA. Stay there. Try not to die. *(Myra laughs.)* I mean it, I haven't finished telling you. *(Jenna leaves. Myra looks around her, smiling quietly. She slowly lies down on her side, and strokes the moss with her hand. She tucks her feet up and places her hands under her face, as if she were asleep. After a few moments, Myra changes her mind. She rolls over slowly and lies on her back, looking up at the sky. Fade.)*

End of Play

PROPERTY LIST

White cardboard coffin
Picnic basket with blanket, plates, utensils, napkins, food
Purse with cigarettes, lighter, phone
Purse with bottle of pills, water
Laptop
Bottle of wine, glasses
Bottle of red wine, glass
Newspaper
Sports bag
Shoes, shoe trees, slippers
Cat food
Tupperware container, fork
Backpack, plastic bag, tissues
Fan heater, screwdriver
Brahms album
Box of spices
Newspaper, pen
Tissues
Chocolate bar
Telephone, piece of paper
Sweater
Pencils
Tic-Tacs, plastic bag
Paintbrush, paint
Handkerchief, book
Business card

SOUND EFFECTS

"Hungarian Dances" by Brahms

NEW PLAYS

★ **THE EXONERATED by Jessica Blank and Erik Jensen.** Six interwoven stories paint a picture of an American criminal justice system gone horribly wrong and six brave souls who persevered to survive it. "The #1 play of the year...intense and deeply affecting..." *–NY Times.* "Riveting. Simple, honest storytelling that demands reflection." *–A.P.* "Artful and moving...pays tribute to the resilience of human hearts and minds." *–Variety.* "Stark...riveting...cunningly orchestrated." *–The New Yorker.* "Hard-hitting, powerful, and socially relevant." *–Hollywood Reporter.* [7M, 3W] ISBN: 0-8222-1946-8

★ **STRING FEVER by Jacquelyn Reingold.** Lily juggles the big issues: turning forty, artificial insemination and the elusive scientific Theory of Everything in this Off-Broadway comedy hit. "Applies the elusive rules of string theory to the conundrums of one woman's love life. Think *Sex and the City* meets *Copenhagen.*" *–NY Times.* "A funny offbeat and touching look at relationships...an appealing romantic comedy populated by oddball characters." *–NY Daily News.* "Where kooky, zany, and madcap meet...whimsically winsome." *–NY Magazine.* "STRING FEVER will have audience members happily stringing along." *–TheaterMania.com.* "Reingold's language is surprising, inventive, and unique." *–nytheatre.com.* "...[a] whimsical comic voice." *–Time Out.* [3M, 3W (doubling)] ISBN: 0-8222-1952-2

★ **DEBBIE DOES DALLAS adapted by Erica Schmidt, composed by Andrew Sherman, conceived by Susan L. Schwartz.** A modern morality tale told as a comic musical of tragic proportions as the classic film is brought to the stage. "A scream! A saucy, tongue-in-cheek romp." *–The New Yorker.* "Hilarious! DEBBIE manages to have it all: beauty, brains and a great sense of humor!" *–Time Out.* "Shamelessly silly, shrewdly self-aware and proud of being naughty. Great fun!" *–NY Times.* "Racy and raucous, a lighthearted, fast-paced thoroughly engaging and hilarious send-up." *–NY Daily News.* [3M, 5W] ISBN: 0-8222-1955-7

★ **THE MYSTERY PLAYS by Roberto Aguirre-Sacasa.** Two interrelated one acts, loosely based on the tradition of the medieval mystery plays. "... stylish, spine-tingling...Mr. Aguirre-Sacasa uses standard tricks of horror stories, borrowing liberally from masters like Kafka, Lovecraft, Hitchock...But his mastery of the genre is his own...irresistible." *–NY Times.* "Undaunted by the special-effects limitations of theatre, playwright and *Marvel* comic-book writer Roberto Aguirre-Sacasa maps out some creepy twilight zones in THE MYSTERY PLAYS, an engaging, related pair of one acts...The theatre may rarely deliver shocks equivalent to, say, *Dawn of the Dead,* but Aguirre-Sacasa's work is fine compensation." *–Time Out.* [4M, 2W] ISBN: 0-8222-2038-5

★ **THE JOURNALS OF MIHAIL SEBASTIAN by David Auburn.** This epic one-man play spans eight tumultuous years and opens a uniquely personal window on the Romanian Holocaust and the Second World War. "Powerful." *–NY Times.* "[THE JOURNALS OF MIHAIL SEBASTIAN] allows us to glimpse the idiosyncratic effects of that awful history on one intelligent, pragmatic, recognizably real man..." *–NY Newsday.* [3M, 5W] ISBN: 0-8222-2006-7

★ **LIVING OUT by Lisa Loomer.** The story of the complicated relationship between a Salvadoran nanny and the Anglo lawyer she works for. "A stellar new play. Searingly funny." *–The New Yorker.* "Both generous and merciless, equally enjoyable and disturbing." *–NY Newsday.* "A bitingly funny new comedy. The plight of working mothers is explored from two pointedly contrasting perspectives in this sympathetic, sensitive new play." *–Variety.* [2M, 6W] ISBN: 0-8222-1994-8

DRAMATISTS PLAY SERVICE, INC.
440 Park Avenue South, New York, NY 10016 212-683-8960 Fax 212-213-1539
postmaster@dramatists.com **www.dramatists.com**

NEW PLAYS

★ **MATCH by Stephen Belber.** Mike and Lisa Davis interview a dancer and choreographer about his life, but it is soon evident that their agenda will either ruin or inspire them—and definitely change their lives forever. "Prolific laughs and ear-to-ear smiles." *–NY Magazine.* "Uproariously funny, deeply moving, enthralling theater. Stephen Belber's MATCH has great beauty and tenderness, and abounds in wit." *–NY Daily News.* "Three and a half out of four stars." *–USA Today.* "A theatrical steeplechase that leads straight from outrageous bitchery to unadorned, heartfelt emotion." *–Wall Street Journal.* [2M, 1W] ISBN: 0-8222-2020-2

★ **HANK WILLIAMS: LOST HIGHWAY by Randal Myler and Mark Harelik.** The story of the beloved and volatile country-music legend Hank Williams, featuring twenty-five of his most unforgettable songs. "[LOST HIGHWAY has] the exhilarating feeling of Williams on stage in a particular place on a particular night…serves up classic country with the edges raw and the energy hot…By the end of the play, you've traveled on a profound emotional journey: LOST HIGHWAY transports its audience and communicates the inspiring message of the beauty and richness of Williams' songs…forceful, clear-eyed, moving, impressive." *–Rolling Stone.* "…honors a very particular musical talent with care and energy… smart, sweet, poignant." *–NY Times.* [7M, 3W] ISBN: 0-8222-1985-9

★ **THE STORY by Tracey Scott Wilson.** An ambitious black newspaper reporter goes against her editor to investigate a murder and finds the *best* story…but at what cost? "A singular new voice…deeply emotional, deeply intellectual, and deeply musical…" *–The New Yorker.* "…a conscientious and absorbing new drama…" *–NY Times.* "…a riveting, tough-minded drama about race, reporting and the truth…" *–A.P.* "… a stylish, attention-holding script that ends on a chilling note that will leave viewers with much to talk about." *–Curtain Up.* [2M, 7W (doubling, flexible casting)] ISBN: 0-8222-1998-0

★ **OUR LADY OF 121st STREET by Stephen Adly Guirgis.** The body of Sister Rose, beloved Harlem nun, has been stolen, reuniting a group of life-challenged childhood friends who square off as they wait for her return. "A scorching and dark new comedy… Mr. Guirgis has one of the finest imaginations for dialogue to come along in years." *–NY Times.* "Stephen Guirgis may be the best playwright in America under forty." *–NY Magazine.* [8M, 4W] ISBN: 0-8222-1965-4

★ **HOLLYWOOD ARMS by Carrie Hamilton and Carol Burnett.** The coming-of-age story of a dreamer who manages to escape her bleak life and follow her romantic ambitions to stardom. Based on Carol Burnett's bestselling autobiography, *One More Time.* "…pure theatre and pure entertainment…" *–Talkin' Broadway.* "…a warm, fuzzy evening of theatre." *–BrodwayBeat.com.* "…chuckles and smiles of recognition or surprise flow naturally…a remarkable slice of life." *–TheatreScene.net.* [5M, 5W, 1 girl] ISBN: 0-8222-1959-X

★ **INVENTING VAN GOGH by Steven Dietz.** A haunting and hallucinatory drama about the making of art, the obsession to create and the fine line that separates truth from myth. "Like a van Gogh painting, Dietz's story is a gorgeous example of excess—one that remakes reality with broad, well-chosen brush strokes. At evening's end, we're left with the author's resounding opinions on art and artifice, and provoked by his constant query into which is greater: van Gogh's art or his violent myth." *–Phoenix New Times.* "Dietz's writing is never simple. It is always brilliant. Shaded, compressed, direct, lucid—he frames his subject with a remarkable understanding of painting as a physical experience." *–Tucson Citizen.* [4M, 1W] ISBN: 0-8222-1954-9

DRAMATISTS PLAY SERVICE, INC.
440 Park Avenue South, New York, NY 10016 212-683-8960 Fax 212-213-1539
postmaster@dramatists.com www.dramatists.com

NEW PLAYS

★ **INTIMATE APPAREL by Lynn Nottage.** The moving and lyrical story of a turn-of-the-century black seamstress whose gifted hands and sewing machine are the tools she uses to fashion her dreams from the whole cloth of her life's experiences. "…Nottage's play has a delicacy and eloquence that seem absolutely right for the time she is depicting…" –*NY Daily News.* "…thoughtful, affecting…The play offers poignant commentary on an era when the cut and color of one's dress—and of course, skin—determined whom one could and could not marry, sleep with, even talk to in public." –*Variety.* [2M, 4W] ISBN: 0-8222-2009-1

★ **BROOKLYN BOY by Donald Margulies.** A witty and insightful look at what happens to a writer when his novel hits the bestseller list. "The characters are beautifully drawn, the dialogue sparkles…" –*nytheatre.com.* "Few playwrights have the mastery to smartly investigate so much through a laugh-out-loud comedy that combines the vintage subject matter of successful writer-returning-to-ethnic-roots with the familiar mid-life crisis." –*Show Business Weekly.* [4M, 3W] ISBN: 0-8222-2074-1

★ **CROWNS by Regina Taylor.** Hats become a springboard for an exploration of black history and identity in this celebratory musical play. "Taylor pulls off a Hat Trick: She scores thrice, turning CROWNS into an artful amalgamation of oral history, fashion show, and musical theater…" –*TheatreMania.com.* "…wholly theatrical…Ms. Taylor has created a show that seems to arise out of spontaneous combustion, as if a bevy of department-store customers simultaneously decided to stage a revival meeting in the changing room." –*NY Times.* [1M, 6W (2 musicians)] ISBN: 0-8222-1963-8

★ **EXITS AND ENTRANCES by Athol Fugard.** The story of a relationship between a young playwright on the threshold of his career and an aging actor who has reached the end of his. "[Fugard] can say more with a single line than most playwrights convey in an entire script…Paraphrasing the title, it's safe to say this drama, making its memorable entrance into our consciousness, is unlikely to exit as long as a theater exists for exceptional work." –*Variety.* "A thought-provoking, elegant and engrossing new play…" –*Hollywood Reporter.* [2M] ISBN: 0-8222-2041-5

★ **BUG by Tracy Letts.** A thriller featuring a pair of star-crossed lovers in an Oklahoma City motel facing a bug invasion, paranoia, conspiracy theories and twisted psychological motives. "…obscenely exciting…top-flight craftsmanship. Buckle up and brace yourself…" –*NY Times.* "…[a] thoroughly outrageous and thoroughly entertaining play…the possibility of enemies, real and imagined, to squash has never been more theatrical." –*A.P.* [3M, 2W] ISBN: 0-8222-2016-4

★ **THOM PAIN (BASED ON NOTHING) by Will Eno.** An ordinary man muses on childhood, yearning, disappointment and loss, as he draws the audience into his last-ditch plea for empathy and enlightenment. "It's one of those treasured nights in the theater—treasured nights anywhere, for that matter—that can leave you both breathless with exhilaration and…in a puddle of tears." –*NY Times.* "Eno's words…are familiar, but proffered in a way that is constantly contradictory to our expectations. Beckett is certainly among his literary ancestors." –*nytheatre.com.* [1M] ISBN: 0-8222-2076-4

★ **THE LONG CHRISTMAS RIDE HOME by Paula Vogel.** Past, present and future collide on a snowy Christmas Eve for a troubled family of five. "…[a] lovely and hauntingly original family drama…a work that breathes so much life into the theater." –*Time Out.* "…[a] delicate visual feast…" –*NY Times.* "…brutal and lovely…the overall effect is magical." –*NY Newsday.* [3M, 3W] ISBN: 0-8222-2003-2

DRAMATISTS PLAY SERVICE, INC.
440 Park Avenue South, New York, NY 10016 212-683-8960 Fax 212-213-1539
postmaster@dramatists.com www.dramatists.com